a map to the human heart

Athena ♡

a map to the human heart copyright © 2018
by Athena Rodriguez.
All rights reserved. No part of this book may be
used or reproduced in any manner whatsoever
without written permission except in case of reprints
in the context of reviews.

www.athenarodriguez.co

ISBN-13:
978-0692178904

ISBN-10:
0692178902

Thank you for letting me dream,
giving me the support I need,
reminding me to breathe,
and inspiring me to think.
Mom you are the embodiment of
grace, love, humility, and selflessness.
I love you.

I

Athena ♡

In my universe
you are a king wanting to be loved
and I'm a queen waiting to give it.

a map to the human heart

I thought you were ordinary
and then
you laughed
and I knew
I'd do
just about anything
to hear
my new favorite sound again.

Athena ♡

I felt as if
my life stopped and started
the moment
I saw an adventure
in those eyes.

a map to the human heart

You had a smile
that dared me not
to fall in love with it.

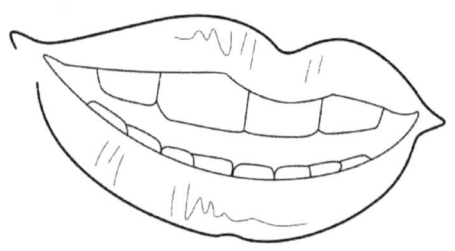

Athena ♡

"Will he be
my best or worst mistake?"

Darling
hope for the best
prepare for the worst.

a map to the human heart

When it's 2 A.M.
and I'm staring at my bedroom ceiling
I want to imagine we are
thinking about each other.

Athena ♡

I want you at night.
I need you in the morning.
And I'd like you
dancing with me in the afternoon.

a map to the human heart

I am afraid of feeling
too much for someone.
I was so afraid of feeling
too much for you.

Athena ♡

The idea of him
made me feel less alone.

You captivated
something inside of me.
And whatever it was
I was hooked.

Athena ♡

When I wake up
I wish to close my eyes
for a bit longer
afraid one night
I won't dream of you.

a map to the human heart

The idea I made about you was
so appealing
so attractive.
You should have seen the life
I planned out.
But it was only a dream.
A really good dream.

Athena ♡

I was blissfully happy
there was just too much excitement
in daydreaming about us.

a map to the human heart

My favorite music playing.
Me laying my head on your chest.
Hearing your heartbeat.
The rain drizzling.

That same dream played so many times.
Too many times.

Athena ♡

I was

    f
      a
        l
        l
          i
            n
              g

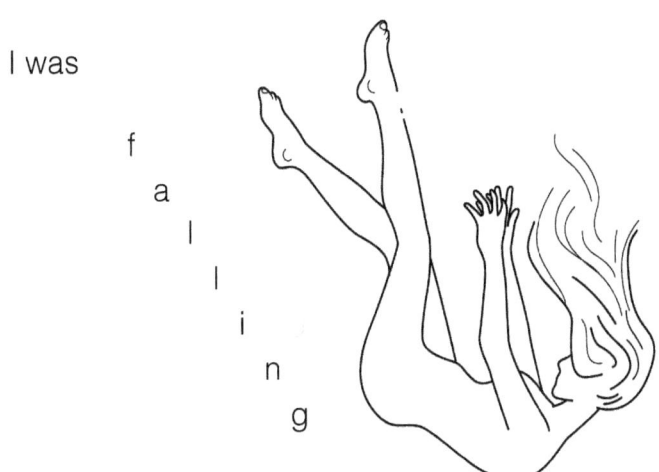

and it didn't matter if
he caught me or not.

a map to the human heart

My heart wants something
my head doesn't need.

Athena ♡

You were the reason
for that big smile on my face.

a map to the human heart

You meant too much to me.
You should have seen how
red my cheeks became
after the mention of your name.

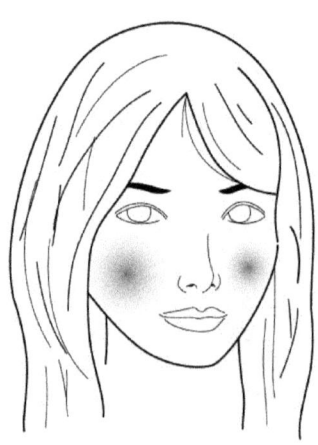

Athena ♡

"Why do girls fall for the wrong guys?"

It's easier than you think.

a map to the human heart

Maybe in another lifetime
I can call you mine.
And we would be together.
You would come to our home
with flowers and sweet promises
of the future.
You would twirl me around
in the kitchen while
dinner was being made.
You would read me my favorite book
under the stars
just before bed
and when I would fall asleep
you'd carry me inside
so utterly happy.
We both would be so happy.
Maybe in another lifetime.
You will be mine.

Athena ♡

I didn't know how
not to make this mistake.

II

Athena ♡

My heart didn't understand
we had no chance with you.

a map to the human heart

The lies dripped from
your lips like caramel.
And I ate every last drop.

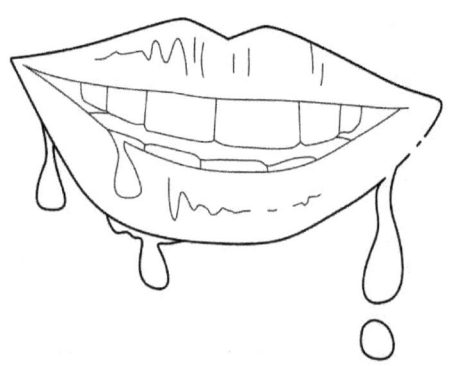

Athena ♡

I was a friend.
A friend to boy
who already had
a person he called home.

But that didn't stop me.

a map to the human heart

Was I even a thought that
crossed your mind?

Athena ♡

It's sad to know
I would have settle
for being
a single thought
inside that body.

a map to the human heart

I am just a friend
and she
well she
was his everything.

Athena ♡

I wonder if he ever looked at me
and wished it was her instead.

a map to the human heart

I would have done
just about anything to hear
"I want you too".

Athena ♡

Can you please
just this once
look at me like I'm more.
Like I mean more.
I want to see the light in your eyes
you get when you're with her.

a map to the human heart

I craved to be the one
that had claimed your heart.

Athena ♡

How lucky she was to have
you wrapped around
her pretty little finger.

a map to the human heart

What a self-deluding fantasy

Athena ♡

wishing to be yours.

a map to the human heart

I wished I had
a map to the human heart
so I'd know the steps to take
to make you love me.

Athena ♡

I could have made you happy.
You know.

a map to the human heart

I was waiting
for someone who would never
need me
want me
or love me.

Athena ♡

How could I blame you?
Some people weren't meant
to love c h a o s.

a map to the human heart

What do I do
when my heart beats for you
and you couldn't care less?

Athena ♡

It sucks doesn't it?
Wanting attention from someone
who doesn't care
whether you come or go.

a map to the human heart

I could have changed everything
about myself
and it still wouldn't be enough.

Athena ♡

It was silly honestly
to believe
I had a chance
to believe
he could have felt the same
to believe
he could have felt anything at all.

a map to the human heart

My heart ached knowing it was losing someone it never had.

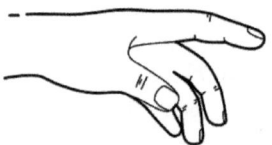 

Athena ♡

I was the only one wanting
to make plans for our future.

a map to the human heart

I wanted to be in love so badly.
But you were just the wrong person
at what felt like the right time.

Athena ♡

You asked
      what my problem was
all I could think was
      "you".

a map to the human heart

I didn't know how much you loved her.
I still don't think
I can truly fathom
the amount you feel for her.
I wanted to be her you know?
I wanted to be the one
to make you smile like that.

Athena ♡

It was hard for me
to understand why you love her.
But it was extremely hard for me
to come up with reasons as to
why you didn't love me.

a map to the human heart

I don't want the thoughts of you
floating around my head anymore.

Athena ♡

Who am I to come between two lovers?

a map to the human heart

I thought I wasn't
good enough for you.
I just wasn't her.
I will never be her
and that's okay.

Athena ♡

Realizing you won't ever love me
the way I expected to be loved
or the way I deserved to be loved
was the wakeup call my heart needed.

a map to the human heart

I think this pain is the worst kind.
Knowing I'm grieving a man
that will never chose me.

Athena ♡

I could have been the one
to mend that broken heart of yours.
And maybe
just maybe
you'd heal mine too.

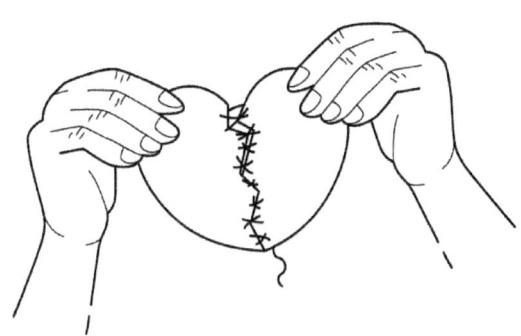

a map to the human heart

It took me awhile
to fully accept that
all the feelings
I had for you
you already felt for her.

Athena ♡

I was left with bittersweet memories
of a man who I loved
but couldn't love me in return.

a map to the human heart

He
was
never
mine
to love.

Athena ♡

I just wanted to be loved.
I think we all just want to be loved.

a map to the human heart

"What hurts?"

Athena ♡

Thinking I had him.
I thought he was
in the palm of my hands.
It hurts to know
I never have and never will have him.

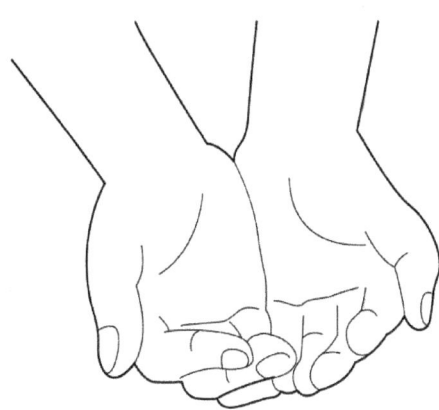

a map to the human heart

Some things will never be worth
the fight.

Athena ♡

There is only so much a person
is willing to take for love.

III

Athena ♡

After him
I picked up what little self worth
I had
And decided it's finally time
to move on.

a map to the human heart

You can not expect somebody
to make you whole.

Athena ♡

I spent too many days
desperately wanting him.
And not enough time
wanting myself.

a map to the human heart

Stop letting him hold so much value in your life.

Athena ♡

My dream used to be you.

Thank goodness I woke up.

a map to the human heart

Everyone has a purpose
and it took me awhile to understand
mine wasn't you.

Athena ♡

Too many of us
have our hearts broken.
Not enough of us
have our hearts cherished.

a map to the human heart

You need to learn to love and
accept yourself
or you will end up devoted to a man
not deserving of you.
All because you were seeking validation
in the wrong things.

Athena ♡

You
don't
need
him
to
bloom.

a map to the human heart

I can and I will
continue to live the rest of my life
without you.

Athena ♡

Wipe the tears.
Pick yourself off the floor.
Look in the mirror.
He is not worth the pain.

a map to the human heart

I have waited a long time to hear
"I love you"
I think I can wait a bit longer.

Athena ♡

Search for the man
that will come
to lift you up
not be the cause of your distress.

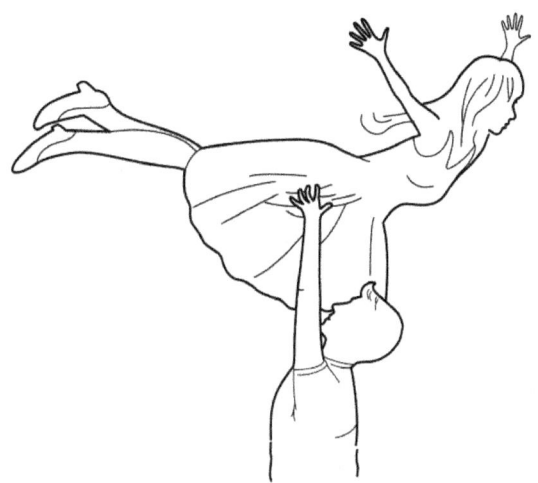

a map to the human heart

I will never again
settle for being
someone's second best.

Athena ♡

Don't plan out love.
Experience it.

a map to the human heart

You deserve to have someone.
And it's okay if that
person is yourself.

Athena ♡

Never suffer in love
only allow it to empower you.

a map to the human heart

I tell myself
I am worth something
and I think it's starting to work.

Athena ♡

I don't want to ever fall in love

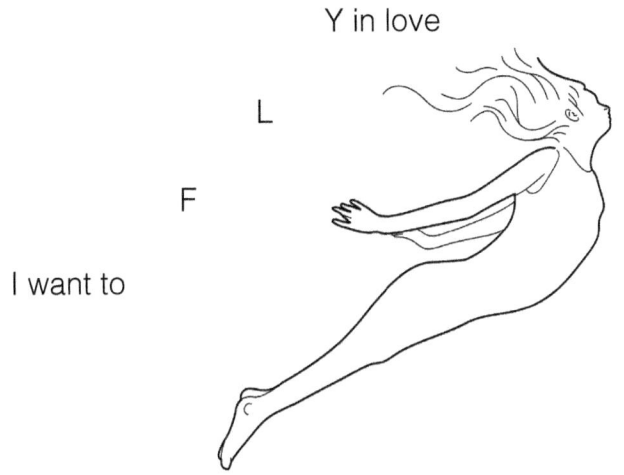

                                        Y in love
                              L
                F

I want to

a map to the human heart

I deserve to be someone's world.
I wasn't made to be a summer evening.

Athena ♡

I have had too much pain
to suffer at the hands of someone
not worthy of my love.

a map to the human heart

If he doesn't choose you
he's a fool.

Athena ♡

She will wake up everyday
and tell herself
she's worthy of love
until she doesn't say it anymore
she knows.

a map to the human heart

I need someone who
recognizes my chaos
names all my storms
understands my volcanoes
and still lets me
brand my name on his heart.

Athena ♡

I think we all have that
once in a lifetime love.
But most of us aren't
patient enough
to wait for it.

a map to the human heart

One day
you will be strong enough
to not rely on stolen glances
from a man that
will never be yours.

Athena ♡

After the pain subsides
you will accept that
he was a lesson
you will learn from.

a map to the human heart

He better look at you like
you are the reason
for him being in this world.

Athena ♡

And with confidence he should know
the world belongs to both of you.

a map to the human heart

He wasn't the one that got away
you were.

Athena ♡

You are a queen
deserving of love
and there is a king out there
worthy enough to love you
and love you the right way.

www.ingramcontent.com/pod-product-compliance
Lightning Source LLC
Chambersburg PA
CBHW061334040426
42444CB00011B/2922